French Lesson

Color & Learn!

Illustrated by

Roz Fulcher

Dover Publications, Inc.
Mineola, New York

This handy book will have you speaking French in no time! More than sixty illustrated pages include commonly used words and phrases in both French and English. Below each French word or phrase you'll find its pronunciation. Syllables in French have equal stress.

Whether it's just for fun, for travel, or to have a conversation with a friend or relative, you'll find out how to talk about the weather, tell what you'd like at mealtime, and many other helpful phrases—and you can color while you learn!

Bibliographical Note

This Dover edition, first published in 2019, is a republication in a different format of the work originally published by Dover in 2015 as *Color & Learn Easy French Phrases for Kids*.

International Standard Book Number

ISBN-13: 978-0-486-83308-8
ISBN-10: 0-486-83308-9

Manufactured in the United States by LSC Communications
83308901 2019
www.doverpublications.com

Bonjour.
bone-zhoor
Good morning.

Salut.
sah-loo
Au revoir.
oh ruh-vwar
Hello. Good-bye.

See you later.

What's your name?

Je m'appelle ____________.
zhuh mah-pell ____________
My name is ____________.

Voici *1. Ma mère* *2. Mon père*

Vwah see mah mare mone pare

3. Ma soeur *4. Mon frère*

ma sur mone frair

This is my 1. Mother 2. Father 3. Sister 4. Brother

Quel age as-tu?
kel ahj ah too
J'ai __________ ans.
zhay __________ ahn
How old are you?
I am ________ years old.

I'm allergic to nuts/eggs.

I love you.

Qu'est-ce qu'on mange au petit-déjeuner?
kess cone mahnzh oh puh-tee deh-zhuh-nay

1. des cereals
day say-ray-ahl

What's for breakfast? 1. Cereal

2. Toast

3. Eggs

1. un sandwich
uhn sahnd-witch

It's time for lunch. I want. . .

1. a sandwich

2. un yaourt
uhn yah-oort

3. un hamburger
uhn ahn-boor-gur

2. Yogurt 3. Hamburger

I'm hungry! What's for dinner?

1. du poulet?
doo poo-lay

2. du poisson?
doo pwa-sone

3. de la pizza?
deuh la pih-zah

1. Chicken? 2. Fish? 3. Pizza?

Qu'est-ce qu'on mange au dessert?
kess cone mahnzh oh duh-sair

Menu

What's for dessert?

1. de la glace
duh lah glahss

2. un fruit
uhn fwee

3. des biscuits
day biss-kwee

1. Ice cream 2. Fruit
3. Cookies

J'aime . . .
zhem
1. Lire
leer
2. Danser
dahn-say
I like to . . .
1. Read
2. Dance

4. Faire de la bicyclette
fair duh la bee-see-clett
3. Dessiner
day-see-nay
3. Draw
4. Bike

2. Pas de quoi.
pah duh kwah
3. Pas de souci.
pah duh soo-seeh
1. Désolé.
day-zoh-lay
1. I'm sorry.
2. Don't worry.
3. It's okay.

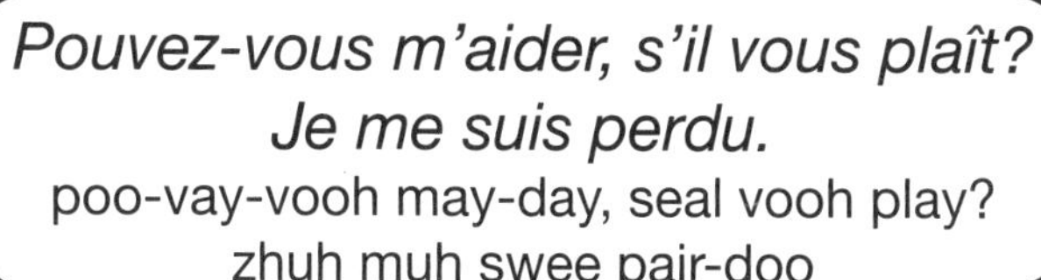

Can you help me, please? I'm lost.

Joyeux Noël!

zhwah-yuh no-ehl

Merry Christmas!

Bonne année!

bone ah-nay

Happy New Year!

This is delicious! I'd like some more.

D'où es-tu?
doo ay-too
Je suis de __________.
zhuh swee duh
Where are you from?
I am from __________.

Les jours de la semaine

Lay joor duh las suh-mehn

Monday — *le lundi*
luh luhn-dee

Tuesday — *le mardi*
luh marr-dee

Wednesday  *le mercredi*
luh mair-kruh-dee

Days of the week

Thursday  *le jeudi*
luh zhuh-dee

Friday  *le vendredi*
luh vahn-druh-dee

Saturday  *le samedi*
luh sahm-dee

Sunday  *le dimanche*
luh dih-manzhe

Les mois
lay mwah
January
February
March
janvier
jahn-vee-ay
fevrier
fay-vree-ay
mars
marze
April
May
June
avril
vreel
mai
may
juin
zhwahn
Months

juillet
zhwee-ay

aout
ooh

septembre
say-tahn-bruh

octobre
ock-toe-bruh

novembre
noh-vahn-bruh

décembre
day-sahn-bruh

Les nombres

lay nohmb

un
uhn

deux
deuh

trois
twah

quatre
kat

cinq
sank

Numbers

six
seese

sept
set

huit
wheet

neuf
nerff

dix
deess

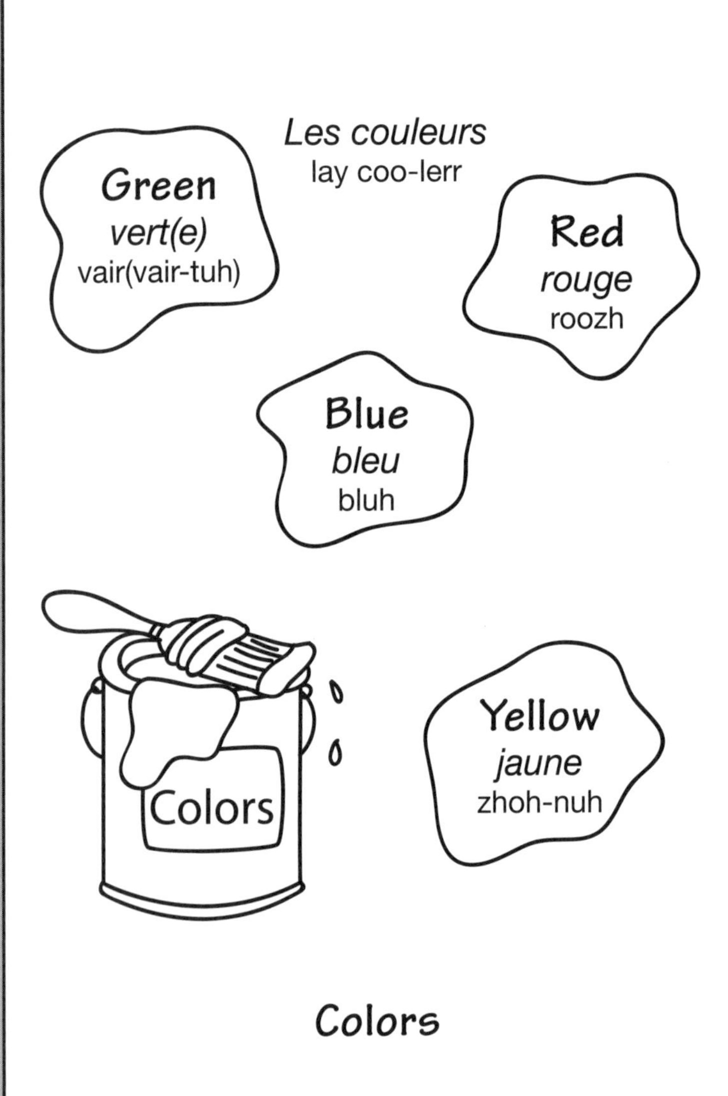
Les couleurs
lay coo-lerr
Green
vert(e)
vair(vair-tuh)
Red
rouge
roozh
Blue
bleu
bluh
Colors
Yellow
jaune
zhoh-nuh
Colors

White
blanc(he)
blahnk(blanshe)

Black
noir(e)
nwahr

Orange
orange
oh-ranzh

Purple
violet(te)
vee-oh-let

Gray
gris(e)
gree(greeze)

1. Allons au parc!
ah-lones oh park
2. Bonne idée!
bone ee-day
1. Let's go to the park!
2. Awesome idea!

1. Combien ça coûte?
comb-bee-yen sah coot
2. C'est un dollar.
set uhn doe-lahr
1. How much does it cost?
2. It's one dollar.

Let's go to the beach! I will get . . .

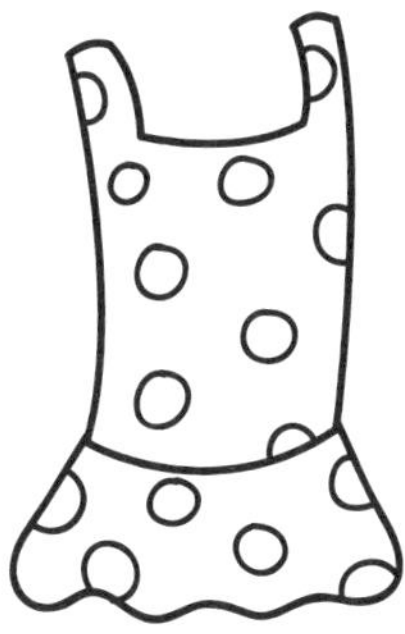

1. mon maillot de bain
mone my-oh duh ban

2. ma lotion solaire
mah lo-see-ohn so-lair

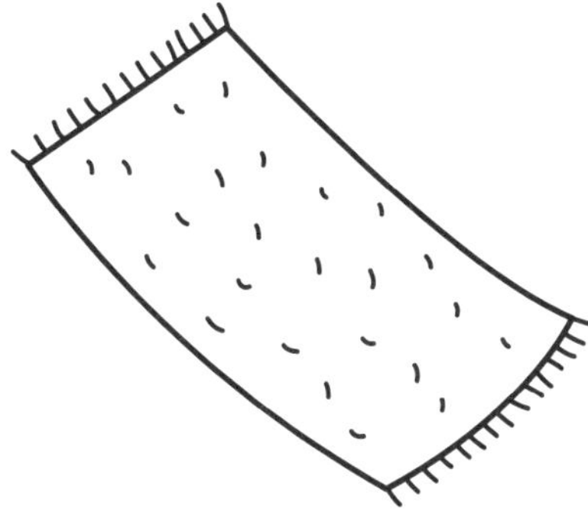

3. ma serviette
mah sair-vee-ett

1. my bathing suit 2. my lotion
3. my towel

Please.

Thank you. You're welcome.

Il pleut. Je prends . . .
eel pleuh. Zhuh prahn
1. mon parapluie
mone pa-ra-ploo-ee
2. mon imperméable
mone ann-pair-may-ahb
It's raining. I'm taking . . .
1. my umbrella 2. my raincoat

Pouvez-vous parler plus lentement?
poo-vay-voo pahr-lay ploo lahnt-moh
Could you speak more slowly?

It's hot today. I'll wear . . .

1. un t-shirt
uhn tee-shurt

2. un short
uhn short

3. des sandales
day sahn-doll

1. a T-shirt 2. shorts
3. sandals

It's snowing! I need . . .

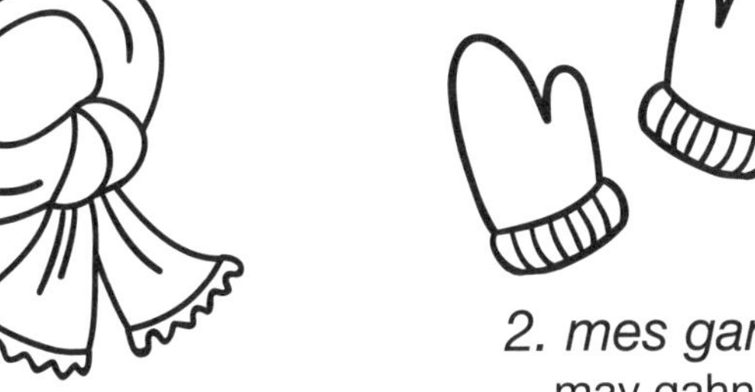

2. mes gants
may gahn

1. mon écharpe
mone ay-sharp

3. mes bottes
may bah-tuh

4. mon manteaux
mone mahn-toe

1. my scarf
2. my gloves
3. my boots
4. my coat

I'm cold. I need . . .

1. un tricot
uhn tree-koe

2. une couverture
oon coo-vair-toor

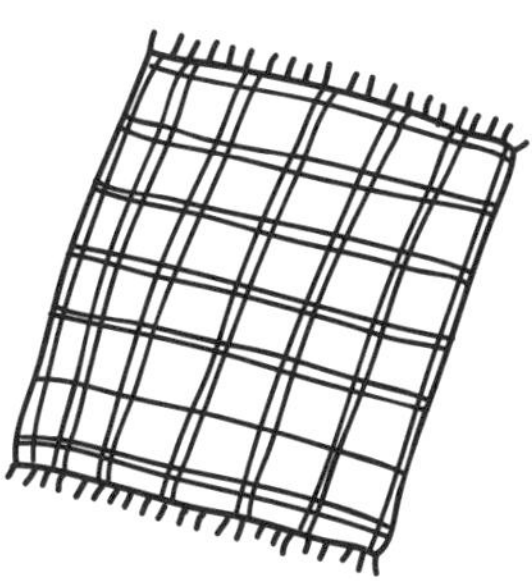

3. une veste
oon vest

1. a sweater 2. a blanket
3. a jacket

Do you speak English?

Sorry, I don't understand.

I'm thirsty. I want . . .

1. de l'eau
duh low

2. du jus
doo zhoo

3. du lait
doo lay

1. water 2. juice 3. milk

Excuse me. Where is the nearest . . .

1. Restaurant?
ress-toe-rahn

2. Arrêt d'autobus?
ah-ray dau-toe-boos

3. Métro?
may-troh

1. restaurant? 2. bus stop?
3. subway?

Tu as un animal domestique?
too ah oon ah-nee-mahl doe-mess-teek?

J'ai . . .
zhay

Do you have a pet? **I have . . .**

1. un chien
uhn shee-yen

2. un chat
uhn shah

3. un poisson
uhn pwah-son

4. un oiseau
uhn wha-zoh

5. un hamster
uhn am-stair

1. a dog 2. a cat 3. a fish
4. a bird 5. a hamster

Happy birthday! My birthday is in

___________.

Can I . . . 1. Watch TV?
2. Go to a movie? 3. Go outside?

Where is the bathroom?

1. Grand-mère
grahn-mayre

2. Grand-père
grahn-pair

3. Tante
Tahn-tuh

4. Oncle
Ohn-kluh

5. Cousine
Koo-zeen

6. Cousin
Koo-zan

1. Grandma **2. Grandpa**
3. Aunt **4. Uncle**
5. Cousin (girl) **6. Cousin (boy)**

J'ai mal à . . .
zhay mahl ah . . .
Je ne me sens pas bien.
zhuh nuh muh sahn pa bee-en
1. la gorge
lah gorge
2. la tête
lah tet
3. l'estomac
lays-toe-mah
I don't feel well. My . . . 1. throat
2. head 3. stomach . . . (hurts)

Je suis fatigué.
zhuh swee fah-tee-gay
Je vais me coucher.
zhuh vay muh koo-shay
I'm tired. Time for bed.

Good night.